Praise for *Jane's Jam*
companion book, *Butter Side Up*

....

2022 Living Now Book Award,
The Evergreen Medal: Silver, Health and Wellnes

"*Butter Side Up: How I Survived My Most Terrible Year and Created My Super Awesome Life* left me emotional from the first chapter. Jane Enright's story of overcoming incredible odds is no short of extraordinary. A story you must read in its entirety to fully grasp, I recommend this book for all readers, especially those who need encouragement in trying times."
—THE SAN FRANCISCO CITY BOOK REVIEW

"Jane Enright has written a brilliant book. This Canadian author has wisdom and insight that helps elevate and empower you! *Butter Side Up* is a must read and one of the best inspirational memoirs to delve in to."
—JOHN BUSBEE, HOST/PRODUCER,
THE CULTURE BUZZ, KFMG 98.9 FM

"Enright is a wonderfully clear-minded narrator of her own experiences.... The result is a stirringly believable tale of personal reinvention. An unsparing, ultimately uplifting account of turning a crisis into a new view of life."
—*KIRKUS REVIEWS*

"An inherently fascinating, inspiring, and deeply personal account, *Butter-Side Up* is exceptionally well written, organized and presented, making it an especially and unreservedly recommended addition to personal reading lists and community library Biography/Memoir collections. With a special appeal to anyone having to deal with sudden loss in their lives, their families, or their careers"
—*MIDWEST BOOK REVIEW*

"Wow, talk about an inspirational but REAL book. Jane tells us how she survived the worst year of her life. . . . She doesn't make it fluffy and rainbows, she makes it real and relatable. This book is a must-read!"

—ASKAWAY BLOG

"*Butter Side Up* is an insightful memoir that draws lessons from Jane Enright's personal challenges."

—FOREWORD REVIEWS

"It's hard to believe that after the heart-wrenching, life-altering curve balls life threw at Jane Enright, she came out on top . . . butter side up. I'm inspired by her story and her optimism!"

—BRAD ARONSON, AUTHOR OF THE NATIONAL
BESTSELLER *HUMANKIND: CHANGING THE
WORLD ONE SMALL ACT AT A TIME*

"The OMG™ strategy is brilliant. I love the feel of the 'outside-in thinking' mindfulness that revolves around the value of gratitude. We're getting a sunny rain shower of bright insights and advice for balance and wellness that delivers much-needed comfort and real talk right now, helping the reader to a better path."

—WRITER'S DIGEST

"What gets me about *Butter Side Up* is how similarly it parallels my own experience dealing with my partner's leukemia treatments. The idea of "sudden, unexpected change can occur rapidly at any moment, hit me like a ton of bricks. It's wonderful how Enright weaves her real-time experiences into this touching tale of love and loss, and caring.

—JARIE BOLANDER, AUTHOR OF *RIDE OR DIE:
A HUSBAND'S MEMOIR OF LOVE, LOSS, AND
THE TRUE MEANING OF COMMITMENT*

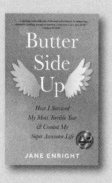

Don't miss *Butter Side Up: How I Survived My Most Terrible Year & Created My Super Awesome Life*

BY JANE ENRIGHT

ISBN: 978-1-64742-075-8

How often have you heard someone say, " I hate change"? That's because most people do. The reality is, whether you like it or not, life puts us all through changes—some challenging, and many joyful—that shape our day-to-day experiences. Sometimes, though, in the blink of an eye, the unthinkable can happen. An event that can change your life forever, and make you ask—"why me'?

Butter Side Up is not self-help jargon; it is edutainment for the soul. Jane Enright's true story of surviving three life-altering events in the span of twelve months, losing almost everything, and coming out the other end stronger and more resilient than ever before is compelling and riveting-and full of sage advice for how to do the same.

With humor, lived experience, and actionable advice, positivity expert and author Jane offers inspiration and hope to readers on accepting unplanned change, building resilience, and landing butter side up in in the game of life. A feel-good story that everyone can relate to and learn from, *Butter Side Up* shows that there can be happiness and joy after unplanned change—and a super awesome life, too.

My Super
Awesome
Life ™

Jane's Jam

Inspiration to Create Your
Super Awesome Life

JANE ENRIGHT

SHE WRITES PRESS

Published 2022
Printed in the United States of America
Print ISBN: 978-1-64742-281-3
E-ISBN: 978-1-64742-282-0
Library of Congress Control Number: 2022913032

For information, address:
She Writes Press
1569 Solano Ave #546
Berkeley, CA 94707

She Writes Press is a division of SparkPoint Studio, LLC.

Photo © Rich Vintage Photography

Contents

························

Prologue xv

Introduction xvii

❋ *Part One: Where Do I Start?*
Begin at the Beginning
(Acceptance & Creating Happiness)

CHAPTER ONE: It Is What It Is 1

CHAPTER TWO: Learning How to Let Go and Accept 5

CHAPTER THREE: The Pursuit of Happiness

(By the way, what time is kickoff?) 9

CHAPTER FOUR: Are We There Yet? 15

❋ *Part Two: What's Next?*
(Outside-in Thinking & Mindfulness)

CHAPTER FIVE: Think BIG (Picture) 25

CHAPTER SIX: Coloring Outside the Lines 29

CHAPTER SEVEN: Learning How to Surf 39

CHAPTER EIGHT: Choosing Peace 43

❋ *Part Three: When You Focus on
the Good in Life, Life Gets Better!
(Gratitude & Kindness)*

CHAPTER NINE: Discovering the Upside
with Gratitude 49

CHAPTER TEN: Saying Thank You Even When it Is
Hard To Do So 53

CHAPTER ELEVEN: Be Your Own Number-One
Draft Pick 61

CHAPTER TWELVE: Self-Care Is Not Selfish 63

CHAPTER THIRTEEN: The Power of You!
Using Your OMG™ 71

Endnotes 75

52 Weeks of Inspiration 79

Suggested Reading 95

Resources To Foster A Sense of Belonging 103

Acknowledgments 107

About the Author 111

For:
Everyone who needs a little inspiration

and

to my family, friends, and Cher who
always inspire & believe in me.

Sometimes it's the smallest decision that can change your life forever.

—KERI RUSSELL

Prologue

....

For Sheena Iyengar and Mark Lepper, it all started with jam.

In the year 2000, the psychologists published a now-famous study about jam and choices.[1] At a gourmet food market, they set up two displays, one with twenty-four varieties of jam and the other with six. They observed that, while shoppers seemed excited about all the options in the larger display, the smaller display ended up selling more product. They concluded that, while more choice seems appealing at first, having too many options can be overwhelming and can paralyze our decision-making process. It appears that when we're faced with too many opportunities for something new, we think there's a greater chance that we won't choose the "best" or the "right" thing, so we don't choose at all rather than risk being unhappy with our decision.

But what if we knew how to not let choice (change) or our fears overwhelm us? What if we could harness the excitement we might initially feel about a new path and then follow through, without allowing ourselves to be stopped by a fear of making a wrong choice or of missing out on a better option? What if we could look at our changing circumstances and see that there is no wrong choice, and there are no mistakes, only an opportunity to discover a new way of being, to learn from our experiences, and to find contentment?

Introduction

....

> *Laughter is the jam on the toast of life.*
> *It adds flavor, keeps it from being too dry,*
> *and makes it easier to swallow.*
>
> —DIANE JOHNSON

For me, it all started with the "tumbling toast" theory.[2] In my book *Butter Side Up: How I Survived My Most Terrible Year & Created My Super Awesome Life* I wrote about how tumbling toast can be a metaphor for change because as human beings, we tend to see the downside rather than the upside when unwanted change happens. And my toast had landed facedown more than once. In the span of twelve months, I had suffered a concussion that left me unable to continue a flourishing career, was forced to rethink my future when my fiancé suffered his own traumatic brain injury, and suddenly lost my best friend of forty years to cancer. With each of those experiences, it became more and more difficult to be optimistic about the future and to believe that there is goodness in life. *And this was before COVID-19 hit.*

But during that year, I also found myself looking for reasons to keep moving forward. There was something deep within me that knew I would find a way through incredible loss and dark times. And I did find a way—three ways, actually: outside-in thinking, mindfulness, and gratitude, or OMG.™ To have an OMG™ approach to life is to understand that embracing change, staying positive, and having faith are the differences between having a super rotten life and a super awesome one, especially during times of trauma and uncertainty.

OMG™ is not about being happy all the time. I am all about positivity, but not the unrealistic or artificial kind. It's important to acknowledge emotions like sadness and anger, and it's okay to sit in the dark for a while. But OMG™ can help you find the light again. *Butter Side Up* is the story of how OMG™ changed my life by helping me successfully navigate the unthinkable and develop a more positive mindset. In *Jane's Jam*, I hope you will learn how to use it to change your life for the better too. I hope you will see that all the jam varieties (choices you have); no matter how many or how few, can bring you sweetness. And that you don't have to be afraid of choice or of bringing something new into your life.

Now more than ever—especially as we deal with the continued stress of COVID—we need positivity and inspiration. We also need proactive, positive strategies to deal with the unexpected. Scholars such as Robert Emmons have scientifically proven that focusing on the good can change our brain chemistry, making us more resilient during times of great stress and major change.[3] *Jane's Jam* is a playbook packed with practical ways to embrace change and new beginnings, especially after a loss, and tips for making OMG™ work for you.

Throughout the course of this book, I will show you how to:

✓ Find courage to look at unexpected change through fresh eyes.

✓ Learn how to let go and accept that things have changed.

✓ Be inspired to discover what you need and truly want to be happy.

✓ Practice using tools that help you create happiness.

✓ Master how to respond objectively—instead of reacting emotionally—to unwanted change.

✓ Practice mindfulness so you can think more optimistically about your past, present, and future.

✓ Explore how to become more resilient to initiate fresh starts and new beginnings

✓ Discover how to use gratitude to find the good when everything is not so good.

✓ Support yourself and others while you recover from unwanted change.

✓ Find courage and motivation to create the super awesome life you deserve.

I've designed *Jane's Jam* as a playbook. Easy to pick up, open to any section, and find something to help you navigate the situation you're in. I have also included ideas, quotes, and some of my favorite passages from my book *Butter Side Up* in the "52 Weeks of Inspiration" section to help you look at change differently in your life and use it to your advantage. Read it. Bookmark it. Mark it up. Give it to a friend. I hope *Jane's Jam* will be a go-to reference for you as you create fresh, new storylines for yourself. I am sharing my experiences and ideas with you because I believe everyone deserves to have a super awesome life—no matter what life throws our way—and that all of us have the capability, on some level, to create it. Let's get started together!

PART ONE

Where Do I Start?
Begin at the Beginning

·····································

> *One day or day one. You decide.*
> —PAULO COELHO

The OMG™ tools I am discussing will be most effective if you do some self-reflection first. The first step is to look inward to determine what might be blocking you from contentment and happiness. I suggest that one of the biggest barriers to happiness is our resistance as human beings to change, particularly the unplanned kind.

Planned change is usually welcomed, a conscious choice or decision, such as picking up a hobby, deciding to marry, or changing careers. Unplanned, unwanted change—like accidents, illness, divorce, pandemics—is the kind that often seems to lack an upside, a reason for happiness. But if we open our minds to the idea that two things can be true at the same time, that something can be heartbreaking or scary but that, on the other hand, endings are opportunities for fresh starts—and also full of potential—we will be able to face it with courage and make it past the discomfort that's inevitable on a journey through the unexpected.

In Part One, we will explore the concepts of acceptance and happiness, and how they can help us on that journey. First, we'll look at what acceptance is, and how to find it when we're faced with challenging situations. Does this mean we have to like the challenging situation? Not always. But we'll be happier if we don't fight it. Then, we will discuss what happiness is (and what it isn't), the importance of a positive mindset, with strategies to approach new beginnings. We will also discuss and practice skills like accepting what is and accepting yourself, the power of affirmations, letting go, and setting a course to create planned change, which is the foundation of looking at choices differently and embracing a more optimistic attitude. When we relax our grasp on the long-term outcomes and focus on the good that can be created during our journey this is when we can experience greater peace and happiness.

CHAPTER ONE

It Is What It Is

....

> *Starting today I need to forget what's
> gone, appreciate what still remains,
> and look forward to what's coming next.*
> —BECKY JOHNSON

Have you ever had to call a game? Had to make a choice you never thought you would have to make, or a decision that you knew was the right one but probably an unpopular one? In 2019, eighteen months after my most terrible year, I made the hardest call I've ever had to make.

After suffering one serious head injury, my fiancé experienced a second, catastrophic one—so catastrophic that he awoke from a ten-day semi coma, unable to remember me or anything about his life or our life together. The doctors said that Clayton might never fully recover from his injuries. Thankfully, he would eventually defy many of their predictions, but his earlier traumas and the aftermath of my own life-altering concussion had already put a strain on our relationship. This time, he would require ongoing intervention that I could not provide. I still loved him, but in my heart, I knew (like in that movie with Robert Redford and Barbra Streisand) that we would never again be the way we were.

What would you do?

I did two things. First, I accepted what had happened for what it was. I didn't like my new reality; I just didn't deny or resist it. I grieved the loss of what Clayton and I had been and what I had wanted us to be, but I didn't dwell on it. Then, after over a year of soul-searching, I decided to end our romantic relationship. I told him I felt that if our lives continued in the same way, I would become resentful of my life rather than grateful for it as I should be, and that would be devastating for both of us.

The next seven months were painful—we had no contact with each other during that time, and some people judged us harshly for the choices we both made. The good news is that, despite this, Clayton and I were willing to try to accept what had happened and let go of the pain. We're still at peace with our choice, and we're still close friends who support and love each other and take care of each other, but in a different way. We are supporting actors in each other's lives, rather than taking the lead. Our ending brought us a new beginning, a joyful new chapter. One that we continue to appreciate with love and gratitude.

Sometimes, facing reality isn't easy. However, I don't want you to pretend that you feel good about something when you don't. It is natural to be disappointed and disheartened when things don't seem to be going the way you feel they should. It is okay to not be okay. Let yourself feel the grief and sadness. But, at a certain point, you can become like a hamster on a wheel and run the risk of becoming comfortable with these negative emotions, making it very difficult to move past them. When this happens, and people get caught in the weeds of discontentment, they prevent themselves from creating new beginnings. Acceptance, which on its face is neutral, is the first step toward letting go of emotions that can bog you down. It's your "go route," as they say in football, to moving forward and creating your super awesome life.

For example, we all have felt the struggle to accept the fact that COVID doesn't seem to be going away. But accepting that COVID is change that can change its mind any time does not mean that you need to be happy about COVID or how it mucked up your plans for how you wanted to live your life. It does mean, though, that you can try to stop resisting the changes it has brought.

Ironically, when we resist the unknown out of fear, that fear of the unknown gets to be in charge of our lives. Acceptance—openness to change—helps us manage our emotional health and helps our minds become more flexible and receptive to pivoting in a new direction. If you accept that rapid unexpected change can happen at any time, and that everyone deserves the right to be happy, you set the stage for using strategies such as outside-in thinking, mindfulness, and gratitude more effectively. You also build a foundation for self-acceptance and discovering your bliss.

As I work through this journey called life, I accept that my life, and every day of my life, is a gift. I accept that, while I cannot control things like the weather or a pandemic, I can control what I think about, how I respond to change, and how I spend my time.

Therefore, acceptance is not looking at the world through rose-colored glasses. It is recognizing the reality of your situation and allowing it to be what it is, without judgment of yourself or others. Accepting that change has occurred helps you move forward, shift your perspective, and develop a more positive mindset. In turn, acceptance can help you become a more flexible thinker and foster your ability to respond to changes productively rather than react to things impulsively, so you can better handle, and look forward to, what comes next.

CHAPTER TWO

Learning How to
Let Go and Accept

*Happiness depends on how you accept,
understand, and surrender to situations.*
—MAYA AMRITANADAMAYI

Accepting the reality of your life sounds like it should be simple enough. But sounding straightforward and being easy to do are different things. Just like any skill, if it's new to you, it takes courage (which you have, even if it doesn't feel like you do), and you also need to practice in order to become proficient at it.. In this chapter, I give you ideas that will help you better understand the concept of acceptance and how to use it to your advantage when making choices. The better you get at accepting change, the less combative you'll feel in the face of it, which puts you in a better position to discover the happiness you are working so hard to have in your life.

ACCEPTANCE GO ROUTES

Acceptance Go Route #1: Five Super Awesome Strategies to Practice Acceptance

Accept yourself. For most of us, self-acceptance can be challenging because we're so used to being our own worst critic. Instead of looking in the mirror and noticing only your flaws, try focusing on what's positive about yourself first. Make a list of your virtues, your talents, your values, your accomplishments. When you keep your strengths in mind, you're more likely to make choices that play to them.

Acknowledge your circumstances. Ignoring or rationalizing your circumstances won't change them. But if you acknowledge your situation, you can ground your goals in reality, making them much more likely to achieve.

Accept that there are no mistakes in life, just lessons. Own your outcomes, even if they are messy. It's a lot easier to mend something if you admit that it's not working. Look at it as a learning opportunity and as a chance to accomplish what's important to you.

Try not to let fear get in your way. Each individual's journey is unique. Don't let fears—especially fear of what others might think of you if you switch gears or take a different life path—stand in your way. You must be willing to do things in ways you think are best for you. Accepting this keeps you from comparing yourself to others as you navigate change. This attitude will help you find the courage you need to make tough choices, but choices that are right for you.

Accept that challenges will always be part of your journey. Don't shy away from challenges, but rather accept that life will always throw us the unexpected. Learning to confront struggles instead of avoiding them builds our resilience. And you never know—sometimes the most challenging experiences provide the most potential for success.

Acceptance Go Route #2: Harness the Power of Positive Affirmations

Author and spiritual teacher Louise Hay built her work on the theory that humans are creatures of habit, that our brains are hardwired for routine, and that our thoughts are merely habitual patterns.[4] She believed that when we change our thoughts and embrace a more optimistic attitude, we can change and improve our circumstances.[5]

Affirmations, or positive self-talk, are a way to change our thinking habits, a guide for our mind using positive words and statements to reframe our perspective. The tipping point is not only thinking that things can be different but feeling it too. This is how we become the quarterback of our life, the individual who makes things happen, rather than the receiver, who waits for things to happen.

Try repeating the following Louise Hay phrases, using your own words, and observe the effect they have on your outlook and emotions over time:

- I have the strength to remain positive in the face of change.

- I am a capable person and can handle anything that comes my way.

- I trust myself to deal effectively with any problems that arise throughout the day.

- I am in the process of making positive changes in all areas of my life.

- I am willing to learn. The more I learn, the more I grow.[6]

Acceptance Go Route #3: Start an "If Things Were Different" Journal

Set aside time each day to write down your thoughts and feelings about a situation in your life (past, present, future) that is challenging to accept. As you're writing, answer these questions: If things were different, and I could move past this event, what would I like to see happen next for me? What would I change for the better? How would I spend my time in a way that benefits me, moves me forward toward my goals, and enriches my life?

CHAPTER THREE

The Pursuit of Happiness
(By the way, what time is kickoff?)

> *It's a hell of a start, being able to recognize what makes you happy.*
> —LUCILLE BALL

Lucille Ball, most famous for her classic TV comedy *I Love Lucy*, had a hell of a sad start. When she was only three years old, her father passed away. And after a bird flew into the room where her family was mourning, she developed what would become a lifelong bird phobia. The following years were unstable too: Her mother remarried, and the family moved several times as they tried to support themselves, at one point having to live with relatives who would not be described as kind. When Lucy was an adult—even though she was a successful, celebrated actress who had won multiple awards— her twenty-year marriage to Desi Arnaz was also rocky.

Does this sound super awesome? No, it does not. But what do we think about most when we think about Lucy? We think about laughter. I don't believe that's coincidental. Lucy used the gift of her sense of humor to rewrite the story of her life and demonstrated that, no matter what we experience, we can choose to laugh and experience joy. As I am writing this, I can picture Lucy in her polka-dot dress with her hands on her hips, standing next to her friend Ethel and saying, "What do you mean I can't have a super awesome life?"

I learned the value of a good sense of humor early on too. From my father. For example, he always has a way of phrasing things that makes me laugh. He used to say, "I don't have a PhD, but I do have a DPE—a Doctorate of Personal Experience." And he once gave me the title of VPCC—Vice President in Charge of Conversation. Turning a familiar thing, like a degree or a title, on its head is funny—and funny defuses tension. And when we reframe something, especially something sorrowful or intimidating, in a funny or even just a positive way, we take away its power to keep us sad or fearful.

During my most terrible year, humor and finding the positive were healing forces for me. They allowed me to promote myself from Vice President in Charge of Conversation to CEO of Everything. I reframed situations that could have defeated me: my head injury, the end of a love affair, and the loss of my best friend to cancer.

Stuff with four letters ending in t happens to all of us, and sometimes it feels like it happens way more than we deserve. No matter how much "stuff" we're facing, though, we can find moments to create happiness. Because it's not what happens to us, it is our reaction to and how we deal with change that affects not only our daily living, but our quality of life in the future. I don't believe that happiness is playing hide-and-seek. We don't have to find it. We can create it through our choices and mindset. I learned that letting go of experiences with humor and grace can help see the way through even the unimaginable, release any negative holds on you, and give you the power to turn negatives into positives with a new chapter. However, just as we learned from the jam choice experiment, choosing something unfamiliar (because we're not used to thinking that happiness is a choice) often takes us out of our comfort zone—that place good or bad, where at least things are predictable.

Often what keeps us from pursuing what we want and need to create a happy, fulfilling, super awesome life is a tendency to believe that past negative experiences mean true happiness isn't possible or available to us. In turn, we sometimes become our experiences: I am divorced. I am unemployed. I am a widow. I was an unhappy child. What if, like Lucy, instead of saying, "I am" or "I was" these things, we said, "These things happened in my life"? What if we saw these experiences as merely events, turning points, or changes, instead of definitions of who we are? Does this mean you shouldn't acknowledge the pain these events caused? No. But if you don't put a permanent label on yourself, the possibilities for creating a new reality become endless. This is when your past becomes a chapter, not the whole book.

Take me, for instance. I was married to a great guy for twenty years, and then we got divorced. It just didn't work out the way we'd planned. While I was married, I had a terrific job as an employment strategist, but my company laid me off. I had to lay myself off from my second career when a concussion made it too difficult for me to continue my work as a strategic planner. After that, the man I thought was going to be my second husband also experienced a traumatic brain injury, one that erased a big part of his memory of our life together. And yes, while we're on the subject of me again, my childhood could have been easier too. Each of these experiences was very challenging, yet each one informed me about who I am. Most importantly, none of them *is who* I am. I am the head coach of my life. I decide who I am and what plays I make. Why wouldn't I want to be the best version of myself? Why wouldn't I do things that make me happy? Why wouldn't you?

✸ ✸ ✸

Happiness and *super awesome* are subjective terms. What makes a musician happy likely isn't what makes an athlete happy. A writer and a biologist probably find joy in completely different situations. But the underlying experience of happiness is pretty universal. Philosophers and scholars have been studying and reflecting on happiness since ancient times. Aristotle asked, "What is the virtue of human existence?" His answer was eudaimonia, or "the essence of humans living well."[7] In her 2007 book *The How of Happiness*, positivity psychology researcher Sonja Lyubomirsky describes happiness as "the experience of joy, contentment, or positive well-being, combined with a sense that one's life is good, meaningful, and worthwhile."

Lyubomirsky's definition suggests that positive feelings lie in internal contentment.[8] This comes from knowing that our life has purpose. I would take it a step further and say that happiness and fulfillment come from acting on that purpose, from using our strengths and talents for our own good and the greater good.[9] Real happiness is an inside job.

Sometimes though, change can knock us for a loop and cause us to question and even rethink our life's purpose, which affects our ability to feel joy. When this happens, we can get back to that happy place by trusting that we know who we are and what our purpose is. And that's easier to do when we accept our circumstances and acknowledge that happiness is a choice.

You are the head coach of your life, and its kickoff time. Make the call to remove the victim label and reframe how you define and talk about yourself. Try making the choice to create happiness, not just find it

CHAPTER FOUR

Are We There Yet?

....

> *Happiness is a direction, not a place.*
>
> —SYDNEY J. HARRIS

Talking about pursuing happiness can feel easier than actually creating it—especially after unplanned change. This is because unwanted change with unpleasant circumstances can interfere with our ability to think positively. Our brains are hardwired to remember and replay things that go wrong.[10] Our thoughts are powerful things and have a ripple effect in all areas of our lives.[11] Negative thoughts often lead to negative, butter-side-down feelings. But the converse is true as well. Positive thoughts usually lead to more positive, butter-side up emotions. I want to reinforce the fact that feelings like sadness and anger are valid. They happen. The key is to recognize when you're stuck in a cycle of negativity and to remember that you have just as much of a right to feel happy as you do to feel unhappy.

It's also important to have and use tools and resources that help us shift our mindset so we can strengthen the connection between positive thoughts and self-talk and the feeling of happiness we want.

HAPPINESS GO ROUTES

Happiness Go Route #1: Know Thyself

The better you know yourself, the more prepared you will be to trust what your life's true purpose is and to accept that experiences in life can help you live that purpose. This self-assessment resource is a great way to begin to reflect on yourself, your current playing field, and what you want to change for the future. By becoming more aware of your feelings and when they happen, you enable yourself to more easily identify what you want to bring in and take out of your life.

SELF-AWARENESS ASSESSMENT

Three goals I have set for myself:

1. _____

2. _____

3. _____

Describe the person that you want to become using three words:

1. _____

2. _____

3. _____

I am happiest when I . . .

_____

_____

_____

_____

_____

_____

_____

_____

Three things that instantly put me in a great mood:

1. _____

2. _____

3. _____

(continued) ▶

▶

I am most unhappy when . . .

_____

_____

_____

_____

_____

_____

_____

_____

_____

_____

_____

_____

_____

_____

_____

One person that makes me feel motivated and inspired:

_____

_____

Two things that make me smile:

1. _____
2. _____

From www.HappierMind.com

Happiness Go Route # 2: Laugh Out Loud

One of the ways we can set a more positive tone after unwanted change is to see the humor in difficult situations, disappointments, and loss. First, laughter is contagious. Some studies suggest that just hearing it triggers something in our brains that makes us want to mimic what we hear.[12] And once we're laughing, we're more relaxed, which makes it easier to resist fear and find the strength to understand and accept difficult circumstances and make decisions. Even the simple act of smiling can affect brain chemistry.[13] No matter what is happening in my life, I try to put a genuine smile on my face at least once a day—as though I'm telling myself in advance, "I don't know what is going to happen today, but I know it's going to be something super awesome!" And you know what? It usually is!

Include laughter in your morning routine. How about adding laughter to your calendar? Schedule time to read a humorous quote or a comic strip, to chat with a fun best friend, or to listen to a podcast that makes you smile.

Learn to laugh at yourself. Most of us take ourselves way too seriously, which limits our ability to find the humor in difficult situations. Granted, sometimes there are situations that are not humorous. However, learning to laugh at yourself takes some of the pressure off, and it will allow you to be more authentic and vulnerable. When you're upset over something, ask yourself: "How is this situation amusing?"

Try something new. When you try or learn something new—like a hobby or a sport—your initial attempts might be clumsy. And let's face it: Awkward is funny. Since you're learning how to laugh at yourself anyway, take up something new. It is likely to result in happy experiences.

Make time to play. Children live to play, purely for the fun of it. Adults tend not to give themselves permission to play because it's "irresponsible." Why, though? Why can't you be responsible and playful at the same time?

Start a happiness jar. Invite family and friends to put their favorite one-liners, stories, anecdotes, or things they love about each other into a jar each week. Read them out loud to each other occasionally and let the laughter and smiles spill out.

Spend time with fun, playful people. There are people who laugh easily—both at themselves and at life's absurdities—and who routinely find the humor in everyday events. Even if you don't consider yourself a humorous person, you can still seek out people who like to laugh and make others laugh. Every comedian appreciates an audience.

Happiness Go Route #3: Find Reasons and Ways to Be Happy (Four Super Awesome Strategies)

See the joy in this moment, no matter how ordinary. Practice not thinking about things you're not doing and savor what you're doing right now, even if it's nothing. Look at the sunset. Enjoy your meals. Marvel at how easy your new hobby has become for you. Joy in the little things is associated with big happiness.

Get involved with people and activities you enjoy. There is ample evidence that having friendships and social support is definitely a source of happiness. Especially with the social restrictions of COVID-19, it's more important than ever to take opportunities to interact with other people as they arise. Even if it's virtual, connecting with colleagues, family, or friends at a dedicated time fosters a sense of belonging and community. Another great way to keep your brain happy is to stay mentally active. This could mean learning to play an instrument or learning to speak a foreign language, or even just challenging yourself with the crossword.

Follow your passion and find your flow. Complete engagement in an activity is called "flow." It should completely absorb your attention and give you a sense of being "in the zone." Perhaps the easiest way to identify a flow experience is that you lose track of time. A flow activity takes skill but isn't too challenging. It should have clear goals and allow you to immerse yourself in what you're doing so your mind doesn't wander.[14] I find my flow in writing, downhill skiing, and yoga. Each activity brings with it a different mindset, but the common denominators are that I lose all sense of time and love the feeling of joy I experience when I am doing these things. By doing or following what you're most passionate about, you are more likely to use your strengths and find a sense of flow.

Create SMART goals. Striving for things we really want can make us feel happy, provided the goals are realistic. Having goals gives life purpose, direction, and a sense of achievement. First consider what you want to achieve, and then commit to it. Set SMART (specific, measurable, attainable, relevant, and time-bound) goals that motivate you, and write them down to make them feel tangible. Break your goal into small steps that you can take one at a time; this will build your self-confidence. Your new reality can begin once you have a plan to move forward with specific goals. Don't forget to celebrate each one as you meet it!

PART TWO

What's Next?

·····························

Now that you have looked inward, it is time to look outward and consider thinking outside-in rather than inside out. Outside-in thinking is big-picture thinking. It helps us see issues from multiple perspectives, develop empathy for ourselves and others, and cope with emotions such as fear and sadness while we navigate change. All of which can lead us to being more mindful and aware of what is happening now, rather than getting caught up in focusing too much on the future or the past.

In Part Two, we will explore the concepts of outside-in thinking and mindfulness (the O and the M in OMG™) and how they can help us. Specifically, we will look at how to respond objectively, rather than reacting emotionally, to unwanted or unplanned change. We'll also delve into how practicing mindfulness can help us think more optimistically about our past, present, and future; why it's important; and how both concepts can allow us to build a foundation that support us to find the resilience to initiate planned change, and create opportunities for a fresh new chapter.

CHAPTER FIVE

Think BIG (Picture)

....

> *Out of crisis comes clarity.*
> —RANDOLPH O'TOOLE

Have you ever found yourself in a situation where everything in your life was running smoothly, and then it happens? Something hits you from so far out in left field that it feels like nothing in your life will ever be the same. You want to crawl far under the covers and never come out again. You feel drained, let down, and overwhelmed to the core.

In my book *Butter Side Up*, I told the story of Jenn, my dear friend of forty years, who went to the hospital with abdominal pain and came out with a terminal diagnosis. Suddenly, she had only weeks to live. What happened to Jenn is an extreme example of massive, unplanned change, but the way she responded to it was a master class, with lessons that any one of us can apply during any kind of unexpected change.

Jenn let herself have her "under the covers" moment; then she chose to respond, rather than react, with outside-in thinking. Out of crisis came clarity. I could hear it in the matter-of-fact way she found her voice, called me, and told me exactly what she needed me to do to help her get through her final days, including the detailed instructions for the party she asked us to have after she passed. What a party it was too, with balloons, a DJ, and dancing. Because Jenn could step outside of herself and say, "This is not my choice, but I accept that this is happening, and this is the support I need from you now." In doing so, we both found the strength and courage to get through it. Using outside-in thinking did not dull the emotional pain, but rather enabled both of us to focus on our gratitude for the blessing of our lifelong friendship. I can feel her on my shoulder now, saying, "Please, Jane, tell the story someday about how we got through it all, and how everyone, including my family, did the best they could."

❋ ❋ ❋

When we are confronted with unwanted change, we often feel powerless. We can become emotionally attached to what was as opposed to being open to what is. But if we accept that change has happened, we reclaim our flexibility of mind because we're more able to use outside-in thinking to move forward as best we can to manage and change our situations for the better.

Outside-in thinking is about looking at your life and your circumstances as an observer rather than as a participant. This allows you to respond to change rather than react to it. It helps you create distance from your emotions—while not hiding or denying them—which eases some of the emotional sting so that you can more clearly visualize the way forward.

Outside-in thinking can not only help us manage our own emotions during change that happens directly to us, but it can also help us better manage the emotions we feel when other people are going through change that makes us, or them feel uncomfortable.[15] Take divorce, for example. According to Albeck and Kayder (2002), women lose about 40 percent of their friendships when they get divorced—particularly those friendships formed during their marriage.[16] The research suggests that the friends who distance themselves do so because they have a hard time getting past what the divorce represents for them—the loss of the dynamic with the previously married couple or the possibility that the same thing could happen to their marriage.[17] Similarly, this can happen when it comes to death and dying. Sometimes, it can be overwhelming for a friend or family member to be close to someone who is dying or who has lost a loved one, so that friend distances themselves to protect their own emotions. But if that person could step outside of the situation and look at it as an observer instead of a participant, it wouldn't feel so threatening. And it would be easier to offer empathy and support to the friend experiencing the change firsthand.

We all have moments when we have to dig deep and find that place where we reconcile what has happened or is happening, come to terms with it, and move forward as best we can. Switching to the role of observer makes this digging easier, bringing us clarity when we need it.

In his book *The Untethered Soul*, author Michael Singer uses a great metaphor to describe the process of outside-in thinking. He says we all have an "inner roommate" who can say harsh things to us, particularly when it feels like our lives aren't going well. He asks us if we would ever allow anyone else to talk to us the way we talk to ourselves. The mere act of imagining someone else saying these things to us is a way to practice outside-in thinking. Outside-in thinking presses the reset button and allows us to better see our behavior from a distance and determine whether it's working for us or against us. If our thinking is more negative in nature, then we can take steps to initiate more positive self-talk which moves our mindsets in a healthier direction.

CHAPTER SIX

Coloring Outside the Lines

....

> *Life is about using the whole box of crayons.*
> —RUPAUL

Outside-in thinking is looking at yourself, others, and situations through a different lens. Imagine you are in the audience watching a play about your life rather than acting in the play. How would you describe what you're seeing in the most objective terms? Another way to think about observing yourself is to imagine you have been asked to do a scan of your life, as though you were a business executive evaluating your company's pros and cons, strengths and challenges. What's working for you, and where might you pivot to be more successful in your changing environment (market)? Effective leaders can step back, envision the outcomes they desire, and make their ideas happen. We can do this in our personal lives if we can get some distance from our emotions. Outside-in thinking lets us color outside the lines. We step outside the box we have put ourselves in and suddenly have the freedom to make choices that challenge the status quo and help us create a joyful life.

In this chapter, I give you tips to help you step back and see yourself and your situation as part of a big picture so you can make choices that help you create the success and happiness you desire.

OUTSIDE-IN THINKING GO ROUTES

Outside-in Thinking Go Route #1: Create a Vision Board

For some people, seeing is believing. A vision board is a physical representation or collage, a snapshot of words and pictures that represent your goals and dreams (planned change). A vision board kick-starts your imagination so that you can bring your dreams to life. It's especially useful for identifying and planning what comes next after unexpected change. The key is to have fun with it. Be playful, be kind, be creative, and think big. And don't forget to use the whole box of crayons when you map out your vision for your super awesome life!

How to Create a Vision Board

1. Think about different areas of your life that you would like to change. Maybe it's your relationship, career, finances, home, social life, spirituality, or personal growth.

2. Handwrite your goals on a piece of paper.

3. Understand that each area need not have the same amount of detail.

4. Using pictures from magazines or the internet, hand-drawn images, or your own photos, create your collage. Organize the images into themes or be more free-flowing—your choice!

5. Write affirmations or key words that describe the feeling you will have when you achieve your goals.

6. Let your creativity shine! For example, if you want to sell your house, take a picture of your house with a SOLD sign and a great selling price. If you are publishing a book, tack up the cover with a five-star critic's rating underneath it. Do you want to play an instrument? Put up a picture of yourself playing it. If you want to adopt a healthy lifestyle, include pictures of yourself being active and photos of nutritious foods.

7. Display your vision board where you can look at it for a few minutes each day and visualize your progress, thinking about how you will feel when you accomplish your goals.

8. Consider pairing your vision board with a journal to track your progress.

Outside-in Thinking Go Route #2: Scan Your Life

An environmental scan, or SWOT analysis, helps you examine the strengths, weaknesses, opportunities, and threats of a situation. An environmental scan is an effective resource to help us look outside in, rather than inside out, so we can focus on the big picture. SWOTS have been a staple in the business world for years. They help organizations decipher what is going well and not so well, so they can successfully navigate change. Similarly, SWOTs can help us initiate and navigate planned and unplanned change in our personal lives. They allow us to examine what is happening now, identify what comes next, and come up with solutions to respond rationally and effectively by helping us focus on strengths, minimize weaknesses, mitigate risk, and take advantage of opportunities and avenues we may or may not have thought of. As you analyze your situation ask yourself these questions:

- What new personal storyline would I like to read about a year from now?

- What perspective and priorities do I want to keep or let go of, as I create my new storyline?

- What intentions can I set that will help me with a fresh start—a new perspective that aligns with my goals and priorities?

- Do I need to make any adjustments to achieve a work–life balance and relationships that are positive and manageable?

- Is there an experience or practice that can help me move forward and live my best life?

How to Complete a Personal SWOT

Visualize the end goal first. No matter whether it is recovering from a layoff, focusing on personal development, or navigating a personal crisis, identifying your end goal(s) makes it easier to see routines, priorities, and areas of focus that require change in order to be successful.

Embrace life as a cycle. Observing yourself—your behavior and patterns—as well as what makes you happy and unhappy from the outside in can help you set intentions that align with positive activities and routines and reinforce your new mindset and goals. Think of shifting your priorities like a cycle; as your life and goals transform, so will your priorities. In other words, scans are living documents that will change over time.

Be honest with yourself. When you're thinking about and answering each quadrant of the SWOT analysis, make an effort to be as honest and comprehensive as possible. You may realize that a strength you possess is more useful for your current goal than you once thought it was, or that an opportunity is now available because of a threat, like a pandemic, that may not have been available before.

Understand that there are no wrong answers. As you complete your SWOT analysis, allow yourself to consider all possibilities. There's no wrong way to envision what you might do next, after an unplanned change.

Use SWOTs during a crisis. Unplanned change can often be prompted by a crisis and require short-term and long-term responses. Once you've accepted that change has happened, ask yourself these questions:

- What initial details do I have about this unplanned change?

- What factors can I control or not control?

- What is the end goal? (short-term)

- Who are key stakeholders? (For example, health care team, family, friends)

- Whom should I stay connected with and how will I communicate with them?

- Who can help me and how can I support myself and others (strengths and opportunities) in this situation? Do I need to fill any gaps (weaknesses and threats) in my network?

- What supports and resources can I access that will assist me in helping myself or others? (For example, friends, family, professionals, support groups, crisis lines, employers, financial institutions, government programs, health care professionals)

- What should I hang onto today, and what should I let go of? (acceptance)

- How will accomplishing this goal help me and others?

- How will I take care of myself today? (strengths and opportunities)

- What will I do today to remain mindful and help me take one day at a time? (See the mindfulness activities in Chapter 8.)

- What are three things I am grateful for today? (see the practicing gratitude activities in Chapter 10)

Use SWOTs for what's next. With the COVID-19 pandemic, many people have experienced or will experience a job interruption, a layoff, or a job loss. A SWOT analysis can help you examine the knowledge you have about a career field (strengths) and what you need to learn (weaknesses). You can also examine the pros and cons (opportunities and threats) of a career field's status in your job market. Gathering this information from the outside in will help you look for opportunities and examine the big picture so you can create a plan for what's next.

Outside-in Thinking Go Route #3: Balance Your Heart with Your Head

Life is full of choices. Some are easy, like what to have for dinner, and others are more complex, such as choosing a career. Regardless of how easy or difficult a decision is, good decision-making skills are useful in life, especially if you feel indecisive about something that is getting you down.

Sometimes it can be challenging to balance your head and your heart while you're making your choice. Your head may be pointing you in one direction (reasoning and logic), and your heart (what you feel) in another. Trusting your intuition (feelings) sometimes means going against the grain and choosing what feels right, rather than what we have been taught to do or what others expect us to do. Acceptance and growth often require us to tap into both: logic and intuition (plus faith that everything will work out as it should). To help balance your thinking and gut feelings, try these strategies:

Ask yourself questions. If I knew that my intuition would help me, what would I want help with? Relationships? Career choices? Personal growth? Financial stability? How would I feel if this area of my life changed for the better?

Weigh your options. Make a list of the pros and cons of a decision so you can make an educated choice.

Don't let stress get the better of you. It's easy to feel stressed and anxious when you're facing a tough choice. You might rush your decisions without thinking them through, or you might avoid making a decision at all because the stress has put you off your game. If you're feeling anxious about a decision, try to manage your stress so it doesn't cloud your thinking. Exercising, taking a yoga class, or spending time with friends can be a great way to manage stress and balance your decision-making

Think about your goals and values. It's important to be true to yourself and what you value in life. When you factor into a decision what is important to you, the best option might become obvious. At any rate, you're more likely to end up with an outcome you're happy with.

Short-list your choices. Just as we learned from the jam choice experiment, the more choices we have, the more challenging the decision-making process can be. Short-listing your choices can help you consider just a few options at a time so you make a more informed decision.

CHAPTER SEVEN

Learning How to Surf

....

> Choose your thoughts carefully. Keep what brings
> you peace, release what brings you suffering, and
> know that happiness is just a thought away.
> —NISHAN PANWAR

If ever there were a story about the power of focusing on the present, it's Bethany Hamilton's. When she was thirteen years old, she was attacked by a shark while she was surfing. She lost her left arm and almost bled to death. Within months of the attack, though, she was back in the water, teaching herself to ride the waves again. Since then, there's been a movie about her experience, and she has launched a company that helps people learn to think and live in healthier, more productive ways.

Bethany is clearly a model for how to reframe tragedy into something positive. I also think she's a great example of what it means to be mindful, which at its core is about choosing to be in this moment. When we're mindful, we can observe memories and feelings about our past as they arise and as thoughts about the future as they occur. However, as I talked about in the outside-in thinking chapters, we can watch these thoughts as they happen but choose not to let them take us with them. If we do get swept into depression over our past or anxious about what might happen in the future, we recognize that we've wandered, and we gently bring ourselves back to where and who we are right now. Bethany could have chosen to live forever in a loop, reliving the trauma of that horrific day in the ocean. But she chooses to see and be where she is right now. "Life is too beautiful to dwell on the wipeouts," she says.

* * *

Just like surfing, focusing on the now—or staying on top of the wave instead of crashing into it—takes practice. Your mind is conditioned to let thoughts and feelings take it wherever they want it to go. Mindfulness helps you break that habit. You learn to regulate your attention so that it stays put while thoughts and feelings wander in and out of your consciousness. The benefits of this are transformational. Just imagine how you would feel without the mental and emotional weight we often carry? Think about it this way: Imagine that you're holding up a full glass of water. It feels light enough, right? But it gets heavier with every minute. What if someone told you that you had to hold it up for an hour? All day? For several days? You'd put that glass down immediately. Yet, we hold onto intangible burdens without question—or even awareness sometimes. Mindfulness helps us stay conscious of what we're carrying and what we're letting ourselves get carried away by. It releases the weight. It doesn't erase our thoughts or feelings or minimize their significance. It merely allows us to easily clear our minds, and when our minds are clear, we're able to make better decisions for ourselves, and take care of ourselves and others more effectively.

Just as you are what you eat, you are what you think—scientists refer to this as experience-dependent neuroplasticity. "Neurons that fire together, wire together," writes Dr. Rick Hanson. "This means that each one of us has the power to use the mind to change the brain to change the mind for the better. To benefit oneself and other beings."[18] In other words, the more we practice mindfulness, the more it becomes a new habit—one that will minimize the effects that things like depression and anxiety can have our well-being.

Take the COVID pandemic, for example. Many people are still wondering when COVID will eventually disappear and let us return to "normal." They are grieving about the past and anxious about the future. For heaps of people, COVID has brought with it the loss of a certain way of life in one way or another. Perhaps the loss of a job or working environment, a relationship, a loved one, or financial stability. On the flipside, we are all in this together. Never in the history of our planet have individuals from every country in the world simultaneously experienced such sudden, rapid, unexpected change. With the unexpected also comes hope and possibilities for change for the better by working together. For example, a layoff can bring with it time and space to consider a new career. Working from home gives us the opportunity for more flexibility and family time. The loss of a loved one is very challenging, but inevitably as human beings, we will all pass at some point; we just don't know when. Sometimes the unanticipated loss of a loved one or hearing about the untimely departure of a friend of a friend gives us cause to pause, clarifies what's essential, and helps us refocus our attention on the relationships that are most important to us. Financially, we can rethink our priorities, rebuild, and start over. As communities, we can come together and find creative solutions to stay together, help, and support each other through troubled times.

Author James Clear once wrote, "The seed of every habit is a single tiny decision." Your mind is a garden, and your thoughts are your seeds. Make the single tiny decision to plant some seeds of optimism and watch how they grow and feed your strength to unburden yourself from the past and see the future as full of possibility. Learning how to surf and ride the tide of unplanned change (like the waves of COVID) with mindfulness can help us enjoy and relish each and every moment of our lives, and create a lifestyle to be cherished and savored.

CHAPTER EIGHT

Choosing Peace

....

> *Nobody can bring you peace but yourself.*
> —RALPH WALDO EMERSON

While I was going through my most terrible year, people kept asking me, "What's your secret to getting through all this?"

I would answer, "I made up my mind to be more mindful and live more intentionally." Every morning, I slowed the busyness and calmed the stress in my brain with meditation, positive affirmations, or yoga. I chose to start my day peacefully no matter what was happening in my life. At the end of my practice, I would say to myself, "I don't know what today is going to bring, but I know it's going to be something super awesome." At the end of my practice, I would say to myself, "I don't know what today is going to bring, but I know it's going to be something super awesome." Choosing to expect the best rather than the worst, focusing on the present, and realizing that the only things I could control were my thoughts, my emotions, and my actions gave me the peace of mind I needed to get through another day of uncertainty.

I still choose to follow this morning routine today. Is every day super awesome all day? No. Do I have to practice keeping my mind in the here and now? I sure do. But the more I practice mindfulness and intentionality, the more resilient I am when negative thoughts start to creep in. Now if something negative is happening, does that mean I ignore it, such as a friend in need, or something that has not turned out the way I want it to go? No. Whatever you are dealing with—whether it's recovering from a trauma or an addiction, grieving the loss of a relationship or a job, or just working on reducing anxiety—a mindfulness routine will keep you focused on what is working well in your life and give your brain a break from chaos.

Below are some activities that will help you live more intentionally in the moment and take things one day at a time so you can be calmer in any kind of storm life sends your way. Be peaceful, be mindful, and be super awesome.

MINDFULNESS GO ROUTES

Mindfulness Go Route #1: Meditate for Mindfulness

Meditation is a strategy for training our minds to become more present. The purpose of meditation is not to cease thinking altogether, but to develop a different attitude about your relationship with your thoughts. Our minds are the most important resource we have. Just as we take care of our bodies with physical exercise, we need to take care of our minds too.

There are many benefits to meditation, including improved brain function, stress relief, and joy. Calming our brains can improve our ability to problem solve, sleep better, and navigate change. Meditation teaches us how to focus our thoughts and emotions on the present, reducing worry and clearing the clutter from our minds so our thought processes and decision-making are clearer. It also helps us celebrate what we do have in our lives rather than focusing on what we don't have.

Sometimes focusing our minds on one thing can seem like herding cats—our thoughts go in seventeen different directions at once. This one-minute mindfulness break from the themindfulmovement.com is a terrific way to reset your mind in the middle of a crisis or just when you need a break—and you can do this brain reboot anywhere:

1. Stop what you are doing, make sure you are in a safe place, and close your eyes.
2. Take a deep breath in through your nose, and breathe out through your mouth.
3. Soften your body anywhere you can, and let go.
4. Without judgment, notice how you are feeling.
5. Repeat deep, intentional breaths for one minute.
6. Open your eyes and go on with your day.
7. Repeat as many times as you need to throughout the day.

Mindfulness Go Route #2:
Find Your Headspace (headspace.com)

It is very easy in our busy world to have your headspace feel crowded. When this happens, it becomes harder to nudge out the negativity and stress in the world around us. I'm a big fan of Andy Puddicombe, a mindfulness and meditation expert and the founder of headspace, an online resource for guided meditations and other mindfulness tools. Andy is a big advocate for protecting your headspace from the harmful effects of stress and anxiety. Check out the headspace.com site for some great resources to become more mindful or try guided meditation.

Mindfulness Go Route #3: Take a Savasana

In yoga practice, the savasana is the final pose, in which you lie on your back, eyes closed, arms and legs outstretched. You breathe naturally and feel the spiritual, mental, and physical benefits of the practice you've just completed. It's a time of stillness and just being. Yoga could be the savasana for your day, a time to center yourself, calm your mind, and just be. Some forms of yoga are a physical workout, some are more about relaxation, and others are a blend. Whatever form you choose—hatha, vinyasa, yoga nidra, etc.—practicing yoga can improve your strength and flexibility and help you sleep better, while aligning your body, mind, and spirit to help you move physically and mentally with more ease through your day.

To get you started with your new routine, try Glo.com or yogawithadrianne.com. These are digital platforms with free voice-guided yoga videos that can help inspire you and get you comfortable with a yoga practice.

PART THREE

When You Focus on the Good in Life, Life Gets Better!

> You can't go back and change the
> beginning but you can start where
> you are and change the ending.
> —C.S LEWIS

In Parts One and Two, we discussed the O and the M in OMG™ and touched a little bit on the G, which is gratitude. In Part Three of *Jane's Jam*, we delve more deeply into the meaning and power of gratitude and kindness. Gratitude is an affirmation of goodness and the foundation for appreciating what you have in life. Kindness is the expression of that gratitude.

In part three, you'll reflect on how kindness—to yourself and others—and gratitude—for yourself and others—are keys to your personal power. You'll explore and practice using tools for finding the good when everything is not so good, and learn how to support yourself and others during healing and recovery from the unexpected. When you focus on the good in your life, your life gets better. The kinder and more grateful you are, the more resilient you are, and the better you can find the courage and motivation to create the super awesome life you deserve.

CHAPTER NINE

Discovering the Upside with Gratitude

···

> *"Look back with forgiveness, forward in hope, downward in compassion, and up in gratitude."*
>
> —ZIG ZIGLAR

Like Bethany Hamilton, legendary Canadian activist Terry Fox was an athlete on the rise when the unimaginable happened. At twenty-two years old, he was diagnosed with a form of cancer that led to the amputation of his leg. It would have been easy for him to put away his running shoes for good. Instead, he did the unthinkable—he learned to run again on a prosthetic limb, and for six months in 1980 ran a twenty-six-mile marathon every day, from Newfoundland to Ontario, raising awareness of and money for cancer research. He ran through snow, rain, wind, heat, and humidity. He stopped in more than four hundred schools, towns, and cities to talk about why he was running. He started at four thirty in the morning and often did not finish his last mile until seven at night. Sometimes Terry and Doug, his best friend and driver, would sleep in their van because they couldn't afford to stay in a motel. Some days hundreds of people cheered him on; other days he was alone on the road and raised no money.

Canadians were deeply inspired by Terry's message of hope, donating millions of dollars to his cause. I was inspired when I saw Terry run through my hometown of Hamilton, Ontario. I admire Terry tremendously for what he achieved and the sacrifices he made to help others—he is my superhero. As I am writing, I think about him because I believe he felt enormously grateful for what he did have. Of course, he mourned what he had lost, but he chose to see the potential in his life and to live the rest of it with gratitude—and that compelled him to do something extraordinary, not only for himself, but for the whole country of Canada, and ultimately for the whole world. The word gratitude comes from the Latin word *gratia*, which means grace, graciousness, or gratefulness. To me, Terry Fox embodied all three of these meanings: He accepted his diagnosis with grace, which gave him the mental space to see beyond his limitations. Terry graciously devoted himself to a greater good because he was grateful for his life, and became a model of how gratitude makes us capable of transforming our lives and the lives of others in ways we never imagined.

Acknowledging and being thankful for our blessings is a way of being kind to ourselves, and when we're kind to ourselves, we are more likely to want to be kind to others. Studies have also shown that repeated acts of kindness release dopamine, the chemical in our brains that can give us a feeling of euphoria. Essentially, the more we treat ourselves and others with kindness, the better we feel. What a wonderful cycle! With the COVID-19 pandemic waves still surging all over the world right now, we have a huge opportunity to practice being thankful and spreading kindness. Yes, we all have experienced profound, sudden losses because of COVID—we've lost family members and friends, financial security, and a sense of physical safety. Still, I believe there is an upside, and that is that we all are experiencing COVID together. We can relate to each other—at least on a basic level—and this empathy can help us work with each other to make the best of our circumstances. I am grateful for the sense of community the pandemic has created, the idea that we are connected to something larger than ourselves. How about you? What will you choose to be grateful for? How will you share your gratitude and kindness with yourself, and the world?

CHAPTER TEN

Saying Thank You Even When It Is Hard To Do So

> "Gratitude makes sense of our
> past, brings peace for today, and
> creates a vision for tomorrow."
>
> —MELODY BEATTIE

Recognizing things to be grateful for after unwanted change, especially change filled with loss, can be challenging. Gratitude won't make you immune to negative feelings, but it can make you more resilient in the midst of change and loss because it magnifies positive emotions rather than negative ones.[19] In their positive psychology studies, researchers Robert Emmons and M.A McCullough and their colleagues have discovered that gratitude is consistently associated with greater, longer-term happiness. They also have determined that people who live with gratitude are more likely to learn and grow in times of stress instead of letting stress overwhelm them.[20]

How can you create a more gratitude-oriented life? Try starting each day by acknowledging one thing that you have to be grateful for—even if it's as simple as the sunshine, the food on your table, or your healthy body. Observe (there's the O in OMG™ again!) how that gratitude makes you feel. Do you feel a shift in yourself? A calming? More contentment? Maybe some of those endorphins are flowing? There are so many things in the world that you can't control, and it can be easy to focus on how those things are taking away from your life. But you can control your reaction to what is happening around you, and I believe that one of the best ways to react is with gratitude. In this chapter, there are some suggestions to get you started so you can find the power of thankfulness and open the door to possibilities with gratitude.

GRATITUDE GO ROUTES

Gratitude Go Route #1: Keep a Gratitude Journal

When we consider that we have a finite amount of time on this planet, we realize that every moment is a gift to be grateful for. Starting your morning with a new routine of gratitude can be a wonderful way to steer your day toward a positive mindset. Listing things you are grateful for daily, and at random, will help you get in the habit of practicing gratitude and being more mindful. Studies show that people who do this feel far less anxious and depressed than people who don't.[21] Begin and end your day with gratitude. Try naming ten things today that you are grateful for.

Gratitude Go Route #2:
Super Awesome Strategies to Practice Being Grateful

Say a kind word. The quickest, simplest, and easiest way to demonstrate gratitude is to say thank you to someone. If you don't have a specific thing to express thanks for, you could just say to someone, "Thank you for being you." Or you could say a few kind words, like "I know you've been having a tough time, and I just want you to know I've been thinking about you." You'll be amazed at how good it feels to say something that makes someone else feel good.

Include others in your plans. Chances are you know someone who is single, alone, or lonely—someone who would really appreciate being part of a group, especially during the holidays. Inviting that individual to accompany you on an outing, share a meal, go for coffee, or take a walk can mean all the difference in the world. When you include others in your plans, it lets them know you're thinking about them and value their friendship. It's also an effortless way to express your gratitude.

Listen intently. Listening is a wonderful gift to give and receive. Showing that you are in the moment in a conversation shows you respect and appreciate the other person.

Take a meal to someone. Whether it's a neighbor, a coworker, friend, or loved one, most people would love to be surprised with a home-cooked meal. I was ever so grateful to receive meals during the more than three months I spent at the hospital advocating and helping loved ones during my most terrible year. A meal made from scratch is a wonderful way to show your gratitude to a person who means a lot to you.

Provide encouragement. We all have people in our lives who are struggling with their self-confidence and questioning whether or not they are capable of completing something they would like to do. Being their cheerleader can help them get past some of their obstacles. Sometimes all it takes is someone else believing in us to help us make our dreams happen.

Perform a random act of kindness. Random acts of kindness are a fun way to spread cheer and joy to others! Here are ten thoughtful kindness ideas from Pinterest.com:

1. Let people merge in front of you in traffic.
2. Take some homemade treats to your neighbor.
3. Surprise your partner/spouse with a warm hug and a compliment.
4. Smile
5. Send a postcard to your parents, children, or grand-children using snail mail.
6. Hide a love note in your spouse's lunch box or briefcase.
7. Reserve judgment and patiently listen to someone's struggles.
8. Hold the door for a stranger.
9. Pay for someone's coffee.
10. Celebrate someone else's good news.

Call to say "Hello." Just like you can thank someone for no particular reason, you can call somebody just to say hello. If that person is having a bad day, they might especially appreciate a kind, easy conversation with a friend. Even if you both are short on time, a brief exchange of pleasantries can stimulate a sense of well-being for both of you.

Ask if there's anything you can do—and actually do it. Like most people, I don't like to ask others for help. Sometimes, however, it is easy to become overwhelmed with all the things on your to-do list, especially as we navigate unplanned change. Since most of us have felt overwhelmed at one time or another, keep an eye out for an overwhelmed friend and ask if there is anything you can do to help—and follow up on your offer if it is accepted.

Send a handwritten note, an email, or a text. A handwritten note is a lovely way to show someone that you care and are thinking about them, or to show your appreciation. If you are busy and can't take the time to handwrite a letter, there is always email. Dash off a thoughtfully worded message to let another person know he or she is in your thoughts. Adding some pictures or entertaining informative items to round out the note is always a great idea too.

Volunteer. Pitching in and volunteering for an afternoon, a day, or on a regular basis at a food bank, shelter, school, community organization, or retirement home is a great way to share your skills, help others, and help your community.

Gratitude Go Route #3: Start a Gratitude Jar

The gratitude jar is a very simple exercise. Yet it can have a priceless, profound effect on your well-being and outlook. It requires only a few items: a jar (a box can also work); a ribbon, stickers, glitter, or whatever else you like to decorate the jar; paper and a pen or pencil for writing your gratitude notes; and gratitude! This can be a great activity for children and families who want to include gratitude as a ritual in their daily living.

STEP 1: Find a jar or box.

STEP 2: Decorate the jar however you wish. You can tie a ribbon around the jar's neck, put stickers on the sides, use clear glue and glitter to make it sparkle, paint it, keep it simple, or do whatever else you can think of to make it look nice.

STEP 3: This is the most important step, which you could do every day: Think of at least three things throughout your day that you are grateful for. It can be something as mundane as a coffee at your favorite place, or as grand as the love of your significant other or a dear friend. Do this every day, if you can: write down what you are grateful for on little slips of paper and put them in the jar.

Over time, you will find that you have a jar full of reasons to be thankful for what you have and to enjoy the life you are living. It also will cultivate a practice of expressing thanks. If you are ever feeling especially down and need a quick pick-me-up, take a few notes out of the jar to remind yourself of who and what is good in your life.

If you need some prompts to get your gratitude ideas flowing, try starting your statements with these phrases:

- I'm grateful for these three things I hear:

- I'm grateful for these three things I see:

- I'm grateful for these three things I smell:

- I'm grateful for these three things I touch/feel:

- I'm grateful for these three things I taste:

- I'm grateful for these three experiences in my life that have brought me wisdom:

- I'm grateful for these three people in my life who have influenced me in a positive way:

CHAPTER ELEVEN

Be Your Own Number-One Draft Pick

···

> Happiness is when what you
> think, what you say, and what you
> do are in harmony.
>
> —MAHATMA GANDHI

O ften when we are going through change in our lives, especially big change, we forget to take care of the most important person in the equation: ourselves! Ideally, you would take time for self-care daily. But you need to believe that you're worth it. Does taking care of yourself first mean you are being self-centered? Not at all. Being your own number-one draft pick, or loving yourself, is not about being self-absorbed or narcissistic. It is about having a high regard and respect for your own well-being and happiness and taking care of your own needs—not sacrificing your well-being for the sake of others. All the things we've talked about in this book so far are forms of self-care. Being objective in your thinking, being mindful, and practicing gratitude are ways of nurturing your physical, psychological, and spiritual well-being.

And during times of unwanted change, it is common for people to feel inadequate. The cure for this is to remember that our value doesn't come from external sources. We are worthy, period, regardless of external judgments. We're worthy even when we don't believe we are. This is where it is important to call on your outside-in thinking, mindfulness, and gratitude skills and be patient with and kind to yourself. Once you have acknowledged your worth, it will become easier to believe you deserve to practice self-care. What that care looks like will be unique to you, but it's an important part of your emotional and physical health.

Whatever being your number-one draft pick means to you, being kind and thankful to yourself is a great starting point for your journey.

CHAPTER TWELVE

Self-Care Is Not Selfish

··

> *How you love yourself is how*
> *you teach others to love you.*
> —RUPI KAUR

We know that self-care can motivate you to make healthy choices in life, but most of us are a better friend to others than we are to ourselves. When you hold yourself in high esteem, you're more likely to choose to say and do things that nurture your well-being. Start by being kind, patient, gentle, and compassionate with yourself, the way you would with someone else you care about. Say "thank you" to yourself and work on developing healthy habits—like eating a healthy diet, exercising, or forming healthy relationships. This includes believing in yourself, trusting your instincts, following your vision, taking action, and being the change, you want to see in the world. It could also include:

- Talking to and about yourself with positive language

- Prioritizing yourself

- Giving yourself a break from self-judgment

- Trusting yourself

- Being true to yourself

- Setting healthy boundaries with others

- Forgiving yourself

- Taking breaks, moving, and exercising

In other words, make a conscious choice to direct your life intentionally, when you can, to create a super awesome lifestyle for yourself and those around you. I say "when you can" because sometimes we are caring for others, like our children or other dependents, and that can make it challenging to make ourselves a priority. Still, carving out time to take care of yourself benefits not only you, but those around you.

SELF-CARE GO ROUTES

Self-Care Go Route #1: Make Yourself a Priority

Take actions based on needs rather than wants. By staying focused on what you need, you turn away from automatic behavior patterns that might get you into trouble or keep you stuck in the past.

Ask for help when you need it. As the adage goes, "A problem shared is a problem halved." Reaching out for support is not a sign of weakness. Rather, by asking for help, you are reducing the burden of a problem on yourself

Respect yourself. Make choices—like spending time with people and on activities that give you energy, eating well, sleeping well, having healthy friendships and healthy intimate relationships—that reflect how much you care about yourself.

Self-Care Go Route #2: Caregivers: Take Care of Yourselves Too

If you are caring for a loved one who is ill or otherwise needs a lot of support, it can be easy to forget about your own needs. Caring for a loved one strains even the most resilient people. You may be so focused on your loved one that you don't realize that your own health and well-being are suffering. People who experience caregiver stress can be vulnerable to suffering declines in their own health. Risk factors for caregiver stress include social isolation, depression, and financial stresses. If you're a caregiver, take steps to preserve your own health and well-being with these suggestions from the Mayo Clinic.

Focus on what you are able to provide. It's normal to feel like you are not doing enough. Believe that you are doing the best you can and making the best decisions you can at any given time.

Set realistic goals. Prioritize, make lists, and establish a daily routine. Don't be afraid to give a raincheck, to decline activities that are overwhelming, such as hosting holiday meals, or to ask others to chip in with activities that lighten the load.

Get connected to resources. Find out about caregiving and health resources in your community. Many communities have classes specifically about the disease your loved one is facing. Caregiving services such as transportation, meal delivery, and housekeeping may be available.

Join a support group. A support group can provide validation and encouragement, as well as strategies and moral support for difficult situations. People in support groups understand what you may be going through. A support group can also be a good place to create meaningful friendships.

Seek social support. Make an effort to stay well-connected with family and friends who can offer nonjudgmental emotional support. Set aside time each week for connecting, even if it's just a walk with a friend.

Set personal health goals. For example, set goals to establish a good sleep routine, find time to exercise on most days of the week, eat a healthy diet, and drink plenty of water. Many caregivers have issues with sleep deprivation. Not getting quality sleep over a long period of time can cause health issues. If you have trouble getting a good night's sleep or must wake often to help a loved one, talk to your doctor and assistance programs for caregivers to help you find time in the day for yourself.

Keep connected with your health-care professional. Get recommended vaccinations and screenings. Make sure to tell your doctor that you're a caregiver. Don't hesitate to mention any concerns or symptoms you have.

Seek out respite care if you need it. It may be hard to imagine leaving your family member or a friend in someone else's care, but taking a break can be one of the best things you do for yourself—as well as the person you're caring for. Most communities have some type of respite care available, and resources can be found on your local town or city website.

Ensure that you have "me" time. Schedule regular time for yourself to enjoy some peace and quiet. Activities such as reading, exercising, yoga and meditation can help you have some R&R so you can recharge your batteries while you care for someone else.

Self-Care Go Route #3: Create an Even More Super Awesome Life with These Self-Care Tips

When you are crafting your super awesome life storyline, don't let someone else write the chapters. Make conscious choices each day that align with your values, beliefs, dreams, and the way you want to live each day.

Live intentionally. Recognize that, despite life's challenges, you can manage how your day will unfold. Our intention creates our reality, and gratitude illuminates the path by helping us stay positive. To help you "tone up" your positive thinking, try including positive affirmations in your daily routine. You can say the following sentences together, or focus on them separately:

- I am choosing to think more positively.

- I am in charge of how I feel today, and I am choosing happiness.

- I am choosing to act and react more positively in challenging situations.

- I have the power to create change.

Our thoughts are powerful things. Living intentionally and being mindful of what you think, feel, and want will help your life reflect this. As Louise Hay said, "Your thoughts are just thoughts, and you have the power to change them."

Take it one day at a time. Taking things one day at a time and staying in the present can help reduce depression about the past and anxiety about the future, especially when a situation like a pandemic brings with it loss and grief. This does not mean you cannot plan for the future; it does mean that you can savor each moment and allow in good things, while still acknowledging what is not so good right now. Take time out each day to clear your mind and just be, even for five minutes. This exercise will help you set your compass for the day and help you choose what you want to let in, or not let in, to your life.

Find your passion. Dream big and believe in the power of you. Think about the absence of something like a relationship, career, or lifestyle as an opportunity to try something new that you are passionate about and that excites and inspires you! Think outside-in to capitalize on opportunities for change and move in the direction of your hopes and dreams. Success means different things to different people, so chart your course in your own way with activities and experiences that bring you up and inspire you.

Pivot. Being an open-minded, flexible thinker will not only attract more brightness into your life, but it can help you successfully handle and navigate change to create your super awesome storyline.

Embrace that life is change and keep moving forward. Any time an unwanted change occurs, say to yourself, "What are the possibilities that this change can bring?"

Develop new routines and rituals. Creating new routines and rituals, especially after change that involves any type of loss, is very important. It helps give us a sense of purpose and helps us recover and move on from loss. Have a standing date night. Get dressed up for dinner. Schedule a virtual family Sunday supper. Make one night a family game night. Develop an exercise routine. Make time for online learning. Schedule free time. Having schedules and routines will help things seem more right side up than upside down.

Recognize your accomplishments. Give yourself an attaboy/attagirl note every day. For example, note how well you handled a situation, that you cleaned the house, exercised, made a great dinner, got your work done, spent a fun afternoon with your children. Anything that will make you smile!

Treat others with kindness and respect. We feel better about ourselves when we treat others the way we hope to be treated. That doesn't mean everybody will always do the same for you, but you cannot control this. Good deeds will always come back to you—and that's positive!

Have fun! When we are stressed, we often try to lose ourselves in other activities such as work. Find time to bring balance to your life and enjoy things like chatting with friends in person or virtually, trying a new recipe, watching a funny movie, or reading a book that inspires you.

Keep the faith. No matter if you are spiritual, religious, or neither, having faith and believing that everything will be okay is an integral part of successfully navigating change. Sometimes the best thing you can do is not think, not wonder, not imagine, and not obsess. Just breathe and have faith and believe that everything will work out as it should.

CHAPTER THIRTEEN

The Power of You! Using Your OMG™

....

> *If you obey all the rules,*
> *you miss all the fun.*
> —KATHARINE HEPBURN

In 1979 author William Bridges wrote, "Every end is a new beginning." This idea underlies everything we've talked about in *Jane's Jam*. If we choose to learn to see unwanted changes as opportunities to write different storylines for ourselves, we strengthen our ability to make it through difficult times, to feel happiness, and to create and live the super awesome life we deserve.

We discussed how letting go of the past with acceptance enables us to welcome new choices and opportunities into our lives. You can ask, "Why me?" It's okay to feel anger, sadness, denial, resentment. Just be aware of when you might be stuck in a self-feeding loop of negative thoughts and emotions. The longer you stay in the cycle, the harder it will be to break out of it.

Giving yourself permission to be the head coach or the CEO of Everything, aka quarterback of your life, can be very liberating—especially during uncertain times, or times in your life when everything seems to be more butter side down than butter side up. It also empowers you to revise your mindset from "life gave me lemons" to "I'm choosing to make lemonade," opening the door to opportunities you never thought possible.

Next we talked about the pursuit of happiness—what it means and choosing to view happiness differently by creating it, rather than finding it—which allows you to view happiness as a direction, not a destination.

Then we discussed thinking big with outside-in thinking. Seeing the world through different eyes—with a more objective lens that helps you take into consideration your own thoughts and emotions, but others too, with compassion and empathy, kindness, and forgiveness—enabling you to envision possibilities and opportunities you never could have imagined before.

Instead of herding cats with your busy brain, you are navigating the journey with your road map called mindfulness—learning how to surf while you ride the waves of change, making up your mind to take things one day at a time in a manageable way by living more intentionally, being careful what you are letting into—or not letting into—your life along the way.

Finally, we discussed the importance, value, and benefits of being grateful and kind to yourself and others. Being grateful and kind illuminates the journey because it is gratitude and kindness that help make our lives easier by allowing us to see the good when it is difficult to do so. This includes making yourself your own number-one draft pick and being kind to yourself. Being your own best friend and creating your super awesome life with choices and habits that are healthy, good for you, and serve you well are what help you help yourself and others.

My intention has been to give you suggestions, ideas for reflection, and activities (go routes) to practice that will help you make healthy choices that are good for you and support you to bounce back more quickly in times of stress and uncertainty. I hope you will consider keeping this book handy and referring to it whenever you need a refresher on how OMG™ can put you back in the driver's seat, which is "way more funner," as my kids used to say, than letting circumstances determine how you feel and behave.

Now, is all this easy? Not always. Changing our habits and moving toward a more positive way of thinking takes practice, time, and space. You might need to delegate—let others help you—and take lots of breaks. You might even need to press the reset button. Starting over when a strategy isn't working isn't failing. It's simply an opportunity to try something that's more effective.

Don't think you have to (or should even try to) change a lot of habits at once. Just like in the jam choice experiment, too many options might be overwhelming. You don't have to obey all the rules either. Consider choosing one OMG™

strategy that makes sense for you at this moment in your life, and practice it at a pace that feels right. Get creative, have fun, and use OMG™ and the go routes as a springboard for your own ideas about shifting your mindset to a more positive, grateful one

I shared these ideas and suggestions with you because I believe it is important to soak up and enjoy every moment we can in life. I also believe we all deserve a super awesome life no matter what. I believe in you. Now it's your turn to believe in yourself. Be like Lucy, Terry, and Bethany. Take something not so good and do the unthinkable. Take a savasana, color outside the lines, break some rules, and leave this planet, and yourself, better than you found it. Go shine—and create *your* super awesome life!

Thanks for hanging in there with me. Until next time, wishing you peace, love, joy , silver linings, and abundant new beginnings. Stay safe and healthy, and stay super awesome!

Warmly,
Jane

Endnotes

....

1. Schwartz, Barry. June 2006. Harvard Business Review. More Isn't Always Better. https://hbr.org/2006/06 /more-isnt-always-better

2. Matthews, R.A.J. (1995). "Tumbling toast, Murphy's Law and the fundamental constants." *European Journal of Physics*. 16(4) 172-176

3. Emmons, Robert, November 16th, 2010, *Greater Good Magazine*, University California at Berkeley

4. https://www.medicalnewstoday.com/articles/320874

5. Hay, Louise, 2004, *I* Can Do It Hay House Inc.

6. Ibid.

7. https://positivepsychology.com/philosophy-of -happiness/

8. https://positivepsychology.com/philosophy-of
   -happiness/puff2018

9. Tartakovsky, 2016

10. Hanson, Rick 2013, *The New Brain Science of Contentment, Calm, and Confidence,* Harmony Press

11. University of Michigan page 129 BSUP

12. source

13. https://www.nbcnews.com/better/health/smiling
    -can-trick-your-brain-happiness-boost-your-health
    -ncna822591

14. Tartakovsky, 2016

15. *Families and Social Networks* by Marylyn Rand, (Sage Publications, 1988). "Changes in Social Networks Following Marital Separation and Divorce" In R. M. Milardo (Ed.)

16. Albeck, S., & Kaydar, D. (2002). "Divorced mothers: Their network of friends pre- and post-divorce" (*Journal of Divorce & Remarriage, 36,* 111-138).

17. Albeck, S., & Kaydar, D. (2002). *Journal of Divorce & Remarriage, 36,* 111-138.

18. Hanson, Rick PhD. With Forrest Hanson, *Resilient: How To Grow an Unshakable Core of Calm, Strength, and Happiness,* 2018, Penguin Books

19. *Greater Good Magazine,* University of California at Berkeley, Robert Emmons, November 16, 2010

20. Emmons RA, McCullough ME. Counted blessings versus burdens: an experimental investigation of gratitude and subjective well-being in daily life. *J Pers Soc Psychol.* 2003;84:377–389. [PubMed] [Google Scholar] [Ref list]

21. Ibid.

52 WEEKS
OF
INSPIRATION

The following quotes are a blend of my favorite thoughts from some of my favorite thinkers as well as excerpts from *Butter Side Up: How I Survived My Most Terrible Year & Created My Super Awesome Life.* I hope you find inspiration in these ideas, as I do.

WEEK 1

"Understand that embracing change, staying positive, and having faith are the difference between having a super rotten life and a super awesome one."

—BUTTER SIDE UP

WEEK 2

"Acceptance is the first step toward successfully navigating change of any kind, especially rapid, unplanned change."

—BUTTER SIDE UP

WEEK 3

It's not about the cards you're dealt, but how you play the hand.

—RANDY PAUSCH

WEEK 4

"Be the change you want to see in the world."
—MAHATMA GANDHI

WEEK 5

"Don't count the days, make the days count."
—MUHAMMED ALI

WEEK 6

"Most people are resistant to change because change takes us out of our comfort zones, that place, good or bad, where we know things are predictable."
—BUTTER SIDE UP

WEEK 7

"Nobody likes a change except a wet baby."
—PETER DRUCKER

WEEK 8

"Remain calm in every situation because peace equals power."
—JOYCE MEYER

WEEK 9

*"Looking at your scenario from the outside
in can help you more readily accept change,
reduce fear, and see the big picture."*

—BUTTER SIDE UP

WEEK 10

*"The first step to getting somewhere is to decide that
you are not going to stay where you are."*

—J.P MORGAN

WEEK 11

*"Having faith that everything will work out
helps you find strength and stay mindful as
you transition through change."*

—BUTTER SIDE UP

WEEK 12

*"When bad things happen, as we try to find
answers, it is very common to internalize our
feelings. Our thoughts are powerful, and people
become a reflection of their thought patterns."*

—BUTTER SIDE UP

WEEK 13

*"Time isn't the enemy. Fear of change is.
Accept that nothing lasts forever and
you'll start to appreciate the advantages
of whatever age you are now."*

—OPRAH WINFREY

WEEK 14

"Good-humor is goodness and wisdom combined."

—OWEN MEREDITH

WEEK 15

*"Success is not final. Failure is not fatal:
it is the courage to continue that counts."*

—WINSTON CHURCHILL

WEEK 16

*"Outside-in thinking helps us not get caught
in the weeds as we navigate change."*

—BUTTER SIDE UP

WEEK 17

"Do every act of your life as though it were the very last act of your life."

—MARCUS AURELIUS

WEEK 18

"In the midst of every crisis lies opportunity."

—ALBERT EINSTEIN

WEEK 19

"Accepting that each individual's journey is unique helps you stay mindful and removes the temptation to compare yourself to others."

—BUTTER SIDE UP

WEEK 20

"Your life does not get better by chance; it gets better by change."

—JIM ROHN

WEEK 21

"Faith is believing in something when logic tells you that you should not."

—MIRACLE ON 34TH STREET

WEEK 22

"Being mindful can help us reduce sadness about the past and anxiety about the future."

—BUTTER SIDE UP

WEEK 23

"You're braver than you believe, stronger than you seem and smarter than you think."

—CHRISTOPHER ROBIN (*WINNIE THE POOH*)

WEEK 24

"Gratitude is a powerful tool that can help us get back on track and stay positive so we can successfully navigate change."

—BUTTER SIDE UP

WEEK 25

"Every one of you has the endurance to achieve what you want to achieve—sometimes you just need a little nudge to keep you going."

—JARIE BOLANDER

WEEK 26

"Gratitude can help us see the upside rather than the downside of situations."

—BUTTER SIDE UP

WEEK 27

"Outside-in thinking helps you visualize and plan the route."

—BUTTER SIDE UP

WEEK 28

"In the end only three things matter; how much you loved, how gently you lived, and how gracefully you let go of things not meant for you."

—BUDDHA

WEEK 29

"Outside-in thinking. Mindfulness. Gratitude—OMG™—is a strategy you can use to successfully navigate change and make your ideas happen, so you can land butter side up in the game of life."

—BUTTER SIDE UP

WEEK 30

"When we are looking for happiness, we often look to others to make us happy. We expect situations and other people to change. However, we cannot change others, control their behavior, circumstances, choices, or decisions. We can only control our own reactions and our own choices, which ultimately change us."
—BUTTER SIDE UP

WEEK 31

"Gratitude can help us develop and maintain a positive perspective while we maneuver any kind of change, especially unplanned change."
—BUTTER SIDE UP

WEEK 32

"Acceptance and OMG™ are your friends in a tough situation. They are tools that can help you find strength and courage to hang on when all you want to do is let go, and let go when all you want to do is hang on."
—BUTTER SIDE UP

WEEK 33

"The happiness of your life depends upon the quality of your thoughts."
—MARCUS AURELIUS

WEEK 34

*"It is our responsibility to shift our
perspective from negative to positive; to define
what we want our life to look like; and to cultivate
a solid life plan to make it happen."*

—BUTTER SIDE UP

WEEK 35

*"Happiness is a choice, one that we
make moment to moment, day by day. Once
you accept this, you don't find happiness—you
create it. Happiness is an inside job."*

—WILLIAM ARTHUR WARD

WEEK 36

*"Everyone is necessarily the
hero of his own life story."*

—JOHN BARTH

WEEK 37

*"We want to be the quarterback of our life.
We want to make our ideas happen, rather
than let things happen."*

—BUTTER SIDE UP

WEEK 38

*"Visualization is essentially using your imagination.
It is a dress rehearsal in your mind for what comes
next. Research has shown that when done well,
visualization techniques can help individuals improve
how they feel and move forward toward their goals,
which is essentially successfully navigating change."*

—BUTTER SIDE UP

WEEK 39

*"Our thoughts are just thoughts,
and we are free to choose new thoughts
and positive thinking any time."*

—LOUISE HAY

WEEK 40

*"Unplanned change with unpleasant
circumstances can often interfere with our
imaginations and our ability to focus on positive
thoughts, rather than negative ones. This is
because as humans, we are programmed to feel
rather than think our way through life."*

—BUTTER SIDE UP

WEEK 41

"It is love and friendship, the sanctity and celebration of our relationships, that not only support a good life, but create one."
—WALLACE STEGNER

WEEK 42

"Being grateful for what you do have instead of focusing on what you don't have helps you stay positive and can illuminate your path as you navigate troubled times."
—BUTTER SIDE UP

WEEK 43

"Fear is a feeling, afraid is a choice."
—JIMI HUNT

WEEK 44

"Understanding the link between your thoughts, feelings, reactions, and actions is important when you are deciding what comes next after unplanned change."
—BUTTER SIDE UP

WEEK 45

"Change is the only constant in life."

—HERACLITUS

WEEK 46

"Mastering the art of positive thinking when you don't know what the next five minutes might bring can be challenging. Positive thinking gives us an extreme advantage during times of extreme stress."

—BUTTER SIDE UP

WEEK 47

"Positive affirmations help us focus on what we can do, rather than what we can't do."

—LOUISE HAY

WEEK 48

"Gratitude can also help individuals increase their sense of self-worth. Once you start to recognize the contributions that other people have made to your life and realize that other people see the value in you—you can transform the way you see yourself."

—BUTTER SIDE UP

WEEK 49

"Gratitude is a powerful tool that helps us develop and maintain a positive perspective, encourages us to move forward, not backward, and can help us stay positive while we figure out our next move after unplanned change."

—BUTTER SIDE UP

WEEK 50

"Just one small positive thought in the morning can change your whole day."

—DALAI LAMA

WEEK 51

"Sometimes the best thing you can do is not think, not wonder, not imagine, and not obsess. Just breathe and have faith and believe that everything will work out as it should."

—UNKNOWN

WEEK 52

"Love recognizes no barriers. It jumps hurdles, leaps fences, and penetrates walls to arrive at it's destination, full of hope."

—MAYA ANGELOU

Suggested Reading

ACCEPTANCE & LETTING GO

You Can Heal Your Life
Louise Hay
Hay House, 2017
The premise of this book is: "Life is really very simple. What we give out, we get back." *Our thoughts create our reality.* By changing the ways in which we think, we can effect tremendous changes in our lives. This notion is not new, but author Louise Hay goes beyond this idea and offers strategies and insights to improve how you think and feel. Its positive and hopeful style will invite you in and instill a sense of confidence and hope.

The Gifts of Imperfection
Brené Brown
Hazelden Publishing, 2010
New York Times best-selling author and professor Dr. Brené Brown shares her thoughts and research on *vulnerability, courage, worthiness,* and *shame,* with ten principals on her

interpretation about the power of Wholehearted Living—a way of engaging with the world from a place of self-worth.

Bearing the Unbearable
Love, Loss, and the Heartbreaking Path of Grief
Wisdom Publications, 2017
Organized into fifty-two short chapters, Dr. Joanne Cacciatore's (love this name), *Bearing the Unbearable* is a companion for life's difficult times, revealing how grief can open our hearts to connection, compassion, and the very essence of our shared humanity.

The Way of Integrity: Finding The Path To Your True Self
Martha Beck
Viking Press, 2021
In the *Way of Integrity*, Martha Beck takes readers on a journey of self-discovery about how as human beings we can use integrity to transform our lives. Using her own personal experiences as a life coach, and scientist, she gives readers a process to let go of life-long patterns of people pleasing, self-sabotage and feeling stuck to help lead you towards your true path and happiness you deserve.

HAPPINESS

Happiness:
1000 + Things Happy Successful People Do Differently
Marc and Angel Chernoff, 2019
In this empowering guide, authors Marc and Angel share the very best insights they've discovered, on topics that include

overcoming setbacks, letting go of what's holding you back, nurturing relationships, finding time for yourself, and cultivating passion in order to achieve your wildest dreams.

Resilient: How To Grow an Unshakable Core of Calm, Strength, and Happiness
Rick Hanson PhD, with Forrest Hanson
Harmony Books, 2018
Encouraging and down-to-earth, author Rick Hanson's step-by-step approach is grounded in the science of positive neuroplasticity. Dr. Hanson shows you how to develop twelve vital inner strengths hardwired into your own nervous system. This book is full of practical suggestions, examples, and insights into the brain. It includes effective ways to interact with others and to repair and deepen important relationships. He explains how to overcome the brain's negativity bias, release painful thoughts and feelings, and replace them with self-compassion, self-worth, joy, and inner peace.

Happiness Is . . . 500 Things to Be Happy About
Lisa Swerling and Ralph Lazar
Chronicle Books, 2014
Classified as a children's book, this lovely anecdotal volume is really perfect for kids and adults of all ages, with inspiration that not only makes you think but celebrates the wonderful moments and sweetness of life.

#Endurance Tweet: A Little Nudge to Keep You Going
Jarie Bolander with Foreward By Mark McGuinness
THiNKaha Books, 2012
This just in time book from my friend and fellow author
Jarie Bolander had me at hello! Filled with encouraging and
insightful anecdotes and ideas, #Endurance will inspire you
with a little nudge we all need from time to time to keep you
going through tough times.

OUTSIDE-IN THINKING

The Live Your Values Deck: Sort Out, Honor, and Practice
What Matters To You Most
Lisa Congdon and Andreea Niculescu
Chronicle Books, 2021
When we make core values guiding principles in our lives
good things begin to happen. This unique self-discovery
resource enables the reader to objectively peruse and reflect
on a 78 card deck of core values that helps identify your core
values and enrich your well-being. A fun, interactive way to
examine not only what matters most to you, but also discuss
with others what matters most to them.

Thinking Fast, and Thinking Slow
Danial Kahneman
Anchor Canada, 2011
Two systems drive the way we think and make choices,
Daniel Kahneman explains: System One is fast, intuitive, and
emotional; System Two is slower, more deliberate, and more

logical. Engaging the reader in a lively conversation about how we think, he shows where we can trust our intuition and how we can tap into the benefits of slow thinking, contrasting the two, to help us assess and make choices that are good for us.

Managing Oneself
Peter F. Drucker
Harvard Business Review Press, 2008
Outwardly a business text, this useful and articulate book can help you complete your inner scan to better identify your strengths, challenges, and what you need to move forward to accomplish your life's purpose.

Blink: The Power Of Thinking Without Thinking
Malcolm Gladwell Back
Bay Books, 2006
Blink is a book about choices that seem to be made in an instant-in the blink of an eye-that actually aren't as simple as they seem. Why some people follow their instincts and win, while others end up stumbling into error? Fascinating read that discusses how our brains really work and why the best decisions and choices are often those that are impossible to explain to others.

MINDFULNESS

The Mindful Movement: themindfulmovement.com
The Mindful Movement strives to facilitate an environment that empowers individuals to live mindfully in all aspects of

their lives. Their website and channel include guided meditations and some fabulous tips about how to be more mindful and live an intentional, happy life. Join Sara Raymond from The Mindful Movement for guided meditations to help you let go of fear and worry and cultivate a peaceful mindset during uncertain times.

Meditation for Fidgety Skeptics
Dan Harris et al.
Penguin Random House, 2019
Too busy to meditate? Can't turn off your brain? Curious about mindfulness but more comfortable in the gym? This book is for you . . .

Start Where You Are: A Journal for Self-Exploration
Meera Lee Patel
Random House, 2015
Start Where You Are is an interactive journal designed to help readers nurture their creativity, mindfulness, and self-motivation. It helps readers investigate the confusion and chaos of daily life with a simple reminder: By taking time to know ourselves and what our dreams are, we can appreciate the world around us and achieve our desires.

Yoga For Beginners App
Yoga is a great way to relax, become more mindful, and melt your stress away. This free workout app is filled with voice-guided workouts that can help you get started. Download at the Apple App store.

GRATITUDE & KINDNESS

Gratitude Works: A 21-Day Program for Creating
Emotional Prosperity
Robert Emmons
John Wiley & Sons, 2013
Recent dramatic advances in our understanding of gratitude
have changed the question from "Does gratitude work?" to
"How do we get more of it?" This book explores evidence-
based practices in a compelling and accessible way and
provides a step-by-step guide to cultivating gratitude
in our lives.

Gratitude
Oliver Sacks
Penguin Random House, 2015 (published posthumously)
During the last few months of his life, Oliver Sacks wrote
a set of essays in which he movingly explored his feelings
about completing a life and coming to terms with his own
death. This heartfelt book is a great read and inspirational
to anyone traversing change. "My predominant feeling is
one of gratitude. I have loved and been loved. I have been
given much, and I have given something in return. Above
all, I have been a sentient being, a thinking animal, on this
beautiful planet, and that in itself has been an enormous
privilege and adventure."

"Want to Be Happy? Be Grateful."
David Stiendal-Rast
TED Talk, November 27, 2013
https://www.youtube.com/ef7194fc-ecdb-4e1c-926c
-0fa866335bf8
In this Ted Talk, Brother David Stiendal-Rast teaches us that
it is not happiness that makes us grateful, but gratefulness
that makes us happy.

A Life of Gratitude
A Journal to Appreciate It All, Big and Small
Chronicle Books, 2013
This uplifting journal is one of my most treasured posses-
sions! Full of insightful, happy ideas to express gratitude with
whimsical illustrations and thoughtful gratitude prompts,
I love this journal and recommend it to any and all. I have
used it for years and use it to write my new moon intentions.

Resources To Foster
A Sense of Belonging

....

We all feel wonderful when we feel a sense of belonging. It might be a place, group of individuals, altruistic activity, volunteering, or membership that brings us together with others, touches our heart and helps us feel special, valued, and happy. Sometimes though when change happens, our connections, routines and rituals change too. This is when it becomes important to revise our habits and ensure we have relationships and activities in our lives that are not only healthy, but nurture our mind, body, soul.

One way to do this is to get involved with organizations that promote beliefs you value such as kindness, inclusiveness, and generosity. Sharing acts of kindness are a fun way to spread cheer and joy, especially during uncertain times. They help us feel better and help those who receive them. Studies by the Greater Good Institute in Berkeley California have "linked" performing repeated acts of kindness to releasing dopamine, a chemical messenger in the brain that can give us a feeling of euphoria". Essentially, we feel better about ourselves when we treat others the way we hope to be treated. While kindness does not make you immune to negative feelings, building relationships with others who feel similarly and work together to make the world a better place can make you more resilient to uncertainty. This is because sharing kindness helps magnify positive emotions rather than negative ones.

Sharing kindness connects and rewards all of us. When we make it a practice to share kindness regularly, not only are we helping others, we are helping ourselves in the process. Kindness is a super awesome way to support our communities and individuals less fortunate to move forward, and stay positive during uncertain times. It also reminds us we are all in this together.

To help you foster a sense of belonging here are some super awesome resources to consider getting involved with who believe in kindness and sharing and leaving the world a better place than they found it.

Alpha Delta Kappa: International Honorary organization for Women Educators
alphadeltakappa.org

Did you ever have an extraordinary teacher that changed your life? One that believed in you and made you feel special, valued, and welcome? Chances are that teacher may have been a member of Alpha Delta Kappa.

Alpha Delta Kappa was founded in 1947 by visionary women who saw a need to recognize and support the professional efforts of outstanding women educators. Alpha Delta Kappa's mission is to empower women educators to advance inclusion, educational excellence, and embrace diversity through world understanding. Since 1947, over 125,000 women educators around the world have discovered the many opportunities provided by membership in Alpha Delta Kappa —opportunities for recognition of commitment to educational excellence, for personal and professional growth and for collectively channeling their energies toward the good of communities, the teaching profession and the world.

And they really mean what they say! As I was putting the finishing touches on Jane's Jam, I was given the extraordinary opportunity to be both a guest and guest speaker at their North Central Region conference. Never have I felt so welcomed and supported by a group of individuals who truly practice what they vision; kindness, generosity of spirit, and altruism in action! I was astounded at the number of community projects that are being supported worldwide by Alpha Delta Kappa including scholarship programs around the globe, Alzheimer's research, mentorship programs for new teachers, and fundraising for education centres...and the list goes on! If you are a female educator looking to establish a sense of community with your peers, and opportunities for professional development which transforms lives Alpha Delta Kappa might be for you!

Bookclubs.com

Fresh ideas for avid readers, book collectors, and curious minds, bookclubs.com enables readers to search our book clubs worldwide and connect with each other to share their love of reading.

Coveyclub.com

Connect with Smart, Interesting Women Just Like You

Covey Clubs meet weekly (or bi-weekly) to discuss common goals or interests. Covey PODs allow you to get to know your Covey sisters in an intimate way, find support, friendship, and a sounding board all at once. They run for 12 weeks, 4 times per year.

Rotary.org

Rotary is a global network of 1.4 million neighbors, friends, leaders, and problem-solvers who see a world where people unite and take action to create lasting change—across the globe, in our communities, and in ourselves. For more than 110 years, Rotary's people of action have used their passion, energy, and intelligence to take action on sustainable projects. From literacy and peace to water and health, they are always working to better our world, and we stay committed to the end. Chapters are located in communities worldwide. For more information visit rotary.org.

Ymca.org/ymca.ca

The YMCA is the leading non-profit committed to strengthening individuals and communities across the country. At the Y, they are here to help you find your "why"—your greater sense of purpose—by connecting you with opportunities to improve your health, support young people, make new friends and contribute to a stronger, more cohesive community for all. YMCA's have organizations all across North America, and internationally. Visit their website for more information about how to get involved.

Acknowledgments

....

Taking a book from start to finish is always a big endeavor, especially two books in one year. I certainly could not have accomplished this without the guidance and support from my truly super awesome and talented editor, Heather Martin from Martin Ink. Heather's outside-in thinking enabled me not only to capture my ideas, but to expand and write about them in a way that I hope will resonate with readers. Thank you, Heather—you are a gift and a pleasure to collaborate with.

Next up a very sincere thank you to Brooke Warner and Lauren Wise at She Writes Press for believing in me and giving me every opportunity to shine as an author. I also need to include a warm shoutout to Crystal, Grace, and Taylor at Spark Point Studios, and to Jane Ubell-Meyer and Lisa Rosenstein at Bedside Reading for helping introduce me, and *Jane's Jam*, to the world.

Finally, I want to thank my wonderful ski sisters (and brothers), Patty, Brenda, Linda, Dave, and Jeff for helping to solve the world's problems on the chairlift at Beaver Valley Ski Club, and Larry and Colin for helping to get our Saturday morning ski group through a cold, cold winter with their wonderful sense of humor and best cocktail recipes ever!

Special love to my friends family and "framily" for their love, support, and laughter; to my adorable new puppy, Cher; and to friends Annabelle and Sue for helping me carve out time to ski and write, and have fun!

The best way to predict the future is to create it.

—PETER DRUCKER

About the Author

Jane Enright is an ordinary person who has survived some extraordinary things. An inspiring and humorous inspirational author, speaker, and positivity expert, Canada-based Enright is a former kindergarten teacher, strategic planner, and university lecturer, as well as the founder and CEO of Everything at My Super Awesome Life Inc. She is also the author of *Butter Side Up: How I Survived My Most Terrible Year & Created My Super Awesome Life.*

Jane speaks to audiences seeking answers to overcoming a fear of the unknown, grief, stress, loss, depression, anxiety, stagnation, indecision, sadness, and more. From top executives to stay-at-home moms, she is helping audiences throughout North America land "butter side up", find joy, successfully manage change and choices, and learn how to create their super awesome life after unexpected change.

You can find Jane on LinkedIn and Instagram, Facebook and Pinterest. For more information, visit her at mysuperawesomelife.com, janeenrightauthor.com, and shewritespress.com

Follow Jane @

mysuperawesomelife.com

janeenrightauthor.com

[swp] shewritespress.com

[IG] janeenright.author

[f] Butter Side Up with author Jane Enright

[P] JaneEnright_Author

[in] Jane Enright

Author photo © Ryan Enright/Ryan Enright Photography

SELECTED TITLES FROM SHE WRITES PRESS

She Writes Press is an independent publishing company founded to serve women writers everywhere. Visit us at www.shewritespress.com.

Falling Together: How to Find Balance, Joy, and Meaningful Change When Your Life Seems to be Falling Apart by Donna Cardillo. $16.95, 978-1-63152-077-8. A funny, big-hearted self-help memoir that tackles divorce, caregiving, burnout, major illness, fears, and low self-esteem—and explores the renewal that comes when we are able to meet these challenges with courage.

Green Nails and Other Acts of Rebellion: Life After Loss by Elaine Soloway. $16.95, 978-1-63152-919-1. An honest, often humorous account of the joys and pains of caregiving for a loved one with a debilitating illness.

Buried Saints: A Memoir by Brin Miller. $16.95, 978-1-63152-509-4. When Brin Miller discovers that her teenage stepson has been sexually abusing her two young daughters, her life is upended and her crumbling marriage shatters completely. But she and her husband, along with their girls, work to learn resilience, forgiveness, strength, and courage, and in doing so, the unimaginable happens: they begin to heal.

Note to Self: A Seven-Step Path to Gratitude and Growth by Laurie Buchanan. $16.95, 978-1-63152-113-3. Transforming intention into action, *Note to Self* equips you to shed your baggage, bridging the gap between where you are and where you want to be—body, mind, and spirit—and empowering you to step into joy-filled living *now!*